INSTANT SERMONS
FOR
BUSY PASTORS

Russell E. Spray

BAKER BOOK HOUSE
Grand Rapids, Michigan 49506

ISBN: 0-8010-8192-0

Seventeenth printing, January 2001

Printed in the United States of America

Contents

Preface 4

1 How Christians Should G-R-O-W (Eph. 4:15) 5

2 How Christians Should Live (II Cor. 5:15) 7

3 The Greatness of Love (Eph. 3:17-19) 8

4 L-O-V-E (I Cor. 13:13) 10

5 Now Is the T-I-M-E (II Cor. 6:2) 12

6 P-R-O-M-I-S-E-S (II Peter 1:4) 13

7 Requirements for God's W-O-R-K (Mic. 6:8) 15

8 The Love of God (Rom. 8:35-39) 17

9 The M-E-R-C-Y of God (Ps. 103:11) 18

10 God's Double Blessings (Eph. 1:3) 20

11 God's Gifts to His Children (Rom. 6:23) 21

12 God Solves Problems (Ps. 34:17) 23

13 Where Is the Joy? (Ps. 51:12) 24

14 What It Means to Be "Born Again" (John 3:3) 26

15 Ways to End Personality Conflicts (Eph. 4:3) 28

16 You Get What You Give (Luke 6:38) 29

17 The Prayers of Righteous Men Prevail (James 5:16) 31

18 The Heavenly Highway (Isa. 35:8) 33

19 Security in Christ (John 16:33) 35

20 Lessons from the Ants (Prov. 6:6-11) 36

21 It's a Must (John 9:4) 38

22 Are You Pulling or Pushing? (I Cor. 10:31) 40

23 Be Your . . . Own Person (I John 4:4) 41

24 Christ and Heaven (I Cor. 2:9) 43

25 A Good Example (Luke 10:25-37) 44

26 With Christ in the Home (John 10:10) 46

27 The Qualities of a Good Mother (Prov. 31:28) 47

Preface

Instant Sermons for Busy Pastors are just that — ready-to-use. To adjust the length of your sermon, simply add as many, or as few, of your own thoughts and illustrations as you wish.

These timesaving sermons may be used by all Christians who speak on spiritual themes — both ministers and lay people.

I pray that all who use and hear them may be blessed.

Russell E. Spray

1

How Christians Should G-R-O-W

"Speaking the truth in love, may grow up into him in all things" (*Eph. 4:15*).

When we are forgiven and cleansed, we are ready to begin making spiritual growth. Following are some of the ways in which Christians should G-R-O-W.

I. G-race
"But grow in grace" (II Peter 3:18).
A. Grace means "favor, kindness, mercy, and forgiveness." God bestows His grace on His children so that they may grow in grace.
B. God's grace provides forgiveness and cleansing (Eph. 2:5). Needs are supplied and blessings received because of God's "grace in his kindness toward us through Christ Jesus" (Eph. 2:7).
C. Christians grow in grace by emulating Christ. They should exude kindness, compassion, forgiveness, and helpfulness as opportunities afford.

II. R-eliance
"In whom all the building fitly framed together groweth unto an holy temple in the Lord" (Eph. 2:21).
A. When Christians depend on their own strength, they fail. Finite power falters, but God's infinite power never fails.
B. Christians grow in stability and steadfastness as they follow the example of Christ. The more like Him they become, the more reliable they will be.
C. In today's troubled world Christians need more and more to rely on the strength Christ gives. "Casting all your care upon him; for he careth for you" (I Peter 5:7).

III. O-bedience
"Desire the sincere milk of the word, that ye may grow thereby" (I Peter 2:2).

A. God's will must become the Christian's desire. If we follow the dictates of our own will, or the will of others in preference to God's will, can we claim to belong to Him?

B. God's Word reveals His will. He enables us to perform His will when we believe and act upon His directions and promises.

C. Christians must desire God's Word if they are to do God's will. Only by wholeheartedly receiving and obeying God's Word can we obtain spiritual growth (II Peter 1:4).

IV. **W-isdom**

"But grow . . . in the knowledge of our Lord and Saviour Jesus Christ" (II Peter 3:18).

A. Failure to grow in wisdom and understanding limits the Christian's outreach for God and helpfulness to others.

B. Christians are promised wisdom. "If any of you lack wisdom, let him ask of God . . . and it shall be given him. But let him ask in faith" (James 1:5-6).

C. Wise Christians glorify God and are a blessing to others. "The wisdom that is from above is first pure, then peaceable, gentle, and easy to be entreated, full of mercy and good fruits, without partiality, and without hypocrisy" (James 3:17). To gain in wisdom is to G-R-O-W in spiritual stature.

2

How Christians Should Live

"He died for all, that they which live should not henceforth live unto themselves, but unto him which died for them, and rose again" (*II Cor. 5:15*).

Many profess to be Christians but fail to live the Christian life. The following points will assist Christians, step by step, to practice what they profess.

I. **Live in Christ**
   "Therefore, if any man be in Christ, he is a new creature" (II Cor. 5:17).
   A. Christians live in Christ. Their sins are forgiven and their guilt has been removed. They are now new creatures in Christ. Old things have passed away and everything is new.
   B. Christ lives within totally committed Christians. His Holy Spirit cleanses and renews them with God's love. They are alive in Christ, and He in them.
   C. Those who live in Christ are directed by the Holy Spirit and strengthened for the challenges of each day (John 16:13).

II. **Live Like Christ**
   "Leaving us an example, that ye should follow his steps" (I Peter 2:21).
   A. Christians have Jesus' example to follow in thinking, hearing, seeing, speaking, doing, and going.
   B. Jesus prayed often, was kind, compassionate, and understanding. He fed the hungry, healed the sick, comforted the bereaved.
   C. Practicing daily prayer, Bible reading, faith, and love helps Christians become like Christ (I Cor. 6:20).

III. **Live for Christ**
   "In every good work to do his will" (Heb. 13:21).
   A. A good soldier lives and sometimes dies for his country. He endures hardships, sacrifices ease and pleasure to protect his land and those he loves.

B. As good soldiers for Jesus Christ, we must be ready to serve, sacrifice, and suffer. Christ gave His life for us. We must live for Him.

C. We live for Christ by denying self and giving Him control of our time, talent, and treasure (II Cor. 5:20).

IV. Live with Christ

"And so shall we ever be with the Lord" (I Thess. 4:17).

A. Christians are privileged to live with the Lord in the here and now, for He has promised to never leave nor forsake His own (Heb. 13:5).

B. Christ is with Christians in this life and He shall also be with them in the life to come. Christ has promised to come again and receive us unto Himself, that where He is there we shall be also (John 14:1-3).

C. We shall live forever with the Lord, where there will be no more sorrow, suffering, or separation. We shall be reunited with redeemed loved ones and be forever with the Lord (II Cor. 5:8-9).

3

The Greatness of Love

"That ye, being rooted and grounded in love, May be able to comprehend with all saints what is the *breadth*, and *length*, and *depth*, and *height;* And to know the love of Christ, which passeth knowledge" (Eph. 3:17-19, ital. mine).

God is love. His love is so great it cannot be fully comprehended. We can only imagine the "greatness of God."

I. Love Is Like the Mountains

"As the mountains are round about Jerusalem, so the Lord is round about his people . . ." (Ps. 125:2).

A. "As the mountains are round about Jerusalem," God's love is broad enough to surround all His children throughout the earth. None need be left out.

8

B. In today's busy and dangerous world there is a lack of personal care and safety. God's love surrounds His people with personal attention and protection.

C. Millions are seeking peace through self effort, the pursuit of pleasure, and possessions. God surrounds His children with confidence and peace. His love is like the mountains (Ps. 72:3).

II. Love Is Like the Rivers
"He that believeth on me . . . out of his belly shall flow rivers of living water" (John 7:38).

A. Like the rivers God's love extends to the far corners of the earth. Rivers flow into the seas to be caught up again and again. Love is eternal, never ending.

B. God's love brings spiritual life and power to everyone who partakes of the Water of Life. It flows through His children to satisfy those who hunger and thirst after righteousness.

C. God's love guides and directs in this life. The next life will lead to the river of life "proceeding out of the throne of God and of the Lamb" (Rev. 22:1).

III. Love Is Like the Oceans
"He will have compassion upon us, . . . and thou wilt cast all their sins into the depths of the sea" (Mic. 7:19).

A. Human love is often fragile, shallow, distorted, and unfaithful. God's love is strong, trustworthy, and dependable — as vast and deep as the ocean.

B. Sinners who repent and accept Christ by faith are forgiven. Their sins are cast into the depths of the sea to be remembered no more.

C. The Holy Spirit cleanses and fills committed Christians with God's love. Love reaches out to share Christ with others (I John 4:7-8).

IV. Love Is Like the Heavens
"For as the heavens are higher than the earth, so are my ways higher than your ways" (Isa. 55:9).

A. God's love is far above our conception of love, as seen when His grace and mercy touches mankind through Jesus Christ (Ps. 108:4).

B. God's love reaches the high and the low, the educated and the uneducated, the rich and the poor. Saturated in His love, all believers are one in Christ (I John 4:4-5).

C. Love will take God's children to heaven when their earthly journey has ended. There shall be no more sin, sorrow, suffering, or separation, "for the former things are passed away" (Rev. 21:4).

4

L-O-V-E

"And now abideth faith, hope, charity [love], these three; but the greatest of these is charity [love]" (I Cor. 13:13)

Included in God's love are goodness, mercy, sympathy, and understanding. Human love produces ardent affection and strong personal attachment. God's love combined with our love brings meaning and purpose to life.

I. **L-ord**

"Thou shalt love the Lord thy God with all thy heart . . . soul . . . mind" (Matt. 22:37).

A. Profession of love for the Lord is futile if words, deeds, and actions indicate a lack of commitment to Him.

B. If the love of possessions, pleasure, and popularity are more important to us than pleasing God, we are still "conformed to this world" (Rom. 12:2).

C. God wants our love without reservation, giving Him first place in our lives, using our time, talent, and treasure for Him (Matt. 19:21).

II. **O-thers**

"Thou shalt love thy neighbour as thyself" (Matt. 22:39).

A. Many people love themselves but fail to love others.

B. We cannot truly love God without loving our fellowman (I John 4:20)

C. We grow in our love by praying with compassion for others. Resentments go when we pray. Helping others and sharing Christ increases love.

III. V-ictory

"But thanks be to God, which giveth us the victory through our Lord Jesus Christ" (I Cor. 15:57).

A. In World War II our freedom was at stake. When the enemy was defeated, the "V" sign became symbolic of victory.

B. Christians are engaged in the greatest battle ever fought. This fight against sin and Satan cannot be won by guns, tanks, or planes, but there is no defense against love.

C. The "V" in love stands for victory because love never fails. Resentments, fear, hatred, and strife come tumbling down when the love of Christ is lifted up.

IV. E-verlasting Life

"God so loved ... he gave his only begotten Son, that whosoever believeth ... should ... have everlasting life" (John 3:16).

A. Faith is necessary for salvation — "whosoever believeth in him." Hope is also needed for successful living. However, in eternity these will no longer have purpose.

B. Most things in this life are fleeting. Houses and cars deteriorate. Youth and beauty fade. Material possessions do not last.

C. Love is eternal. "God is love." Heaven will be permeated by His presence and love. "For the former things are passed away" (Rev. 21:4).

5

Now Is the T-I-M-E

"Behold, now is the accepted time; behold, now is the day of salvation" (II Cor. 6:2).

Now is the time to give our attention to the things of God.

I. T-urn to the Lord
"That they should repent and turn to God" (Acts 26:20).
- A. Now is the time to turn to the Lord. Millions are turning to education, sciences, and psychology only to become more frustrated. Christ alone is the answer to earth's problems.
- B. God often works through other people — doctors, lawyers, loved ones, friends — but our ultimate help must come from the Lord. Trust Him.
- C. Forgiveness and cleansing are ours when we repent and commit our life to God (I John 1:9). Now is the time to keep our eyes on Christ (Heb. 12:2).

II. I-nvest in the Lord
"Lay up for yourselves treasures in heaven . . . for where your treasure is, there will your heart be also" (Matt. 6:20-21).
- A. Millions are investing in temporal possessions — houses, cars, gadgets galore; they pursue things that wear out, rust, and decay.
- B. God demands first place in our life. He expects us to be faithful in worship and to help finance the needs and outreach of the church.
- C. We invest in the Lord when we work for the salvation of souls. Earthly treasures do not last, but spiritual treasures are of eternal value (I Tim. 6:17).

III. M-arch with the Lord
"Thou therefore endure hardness, as a good soldier of Jesus Christ" (II Tim. 2:3).
- A. A good soldier is loyal, denying himself of personal pleasure and profit. He must march, enduring hardship for the love and protection of his country.

B. Now is the time for Christians to advance as good soldiers of Jesus Christ. Sacrifice, loyalty, courage, and love are needed.

C. March with the Lord. Witness to the unsaved of His saving, sanctifying, satisfying, sustaining, and stabilizing power (II Tim. 2:2).

IV. E-ndure for the Lord

"But he that shall endure unto the end, the same shall be saved" (Matt. 24:13).

A. Too often Christians give up when contrary winds blow and storm clouds arise.

B. We need never give up in despair. When shaken and disturbed, hold on to Christ. When we slip, His hand will steady and strengthen us.

C. Christians who endure for the Lord in this life shall rejoice with Him in the life to come (Rev. 2:10).

6

P-R-O-M-I-S-E-S

"Whereby are given unto us exceeding great and precious promises: that by these ye might be partakers of the divine nature, having escaped the corruption that is in the world through lust" (II Peter 1:4).

People often fail to keep their promises, causing hurt and disappointment. God's promises are always kept. He never lets us down.

I. P-eace of Mind

"My peace I give unto you . . . . Let not your heart be troubled" (John 14:27).

A. Peace in today's world is practically unknown. Greed, suspicion, lack of brotherly love, and hunger for power prevent real and lasting peace.

B. God promises peace of mind and heart to those who trust Him. "Thou wilt keep him in perfect peace, whose mind is stayed on thee" (Isa. 26:3).

II. R-est from Labor

"Come unto me, all ye that labour . . . and I will give you rest" (Matt. 11:28).

A. We live in a restless age of much "busy-ness" and little leisure or "time to live." Timesaving gadgets fail to solve the problem.

B. Jesus promised rest from the strain and worry of life if we will cast our care on Him and wait patiently for Him (Ps. 37:7).

III. O-pportunity for Service

"I have set before thee an open door, and no man can shut it" Rev. 3:8).

A. Selfish interests too often deter us from walking through God's door of opportunity to be "workers with him."

B. When we take or make time to do God's work, He has promised to supply the strength, courage, and opportunity (Phil. 4:13, 19).

IV. M-ercy in Need

"That we obtain mercy, and find grace to help in time of need" (Heb. 4:16).

A. Being human, Christians make blunders and flounder many times. But God's mercy is available to reinstate us.

B. God promises grace to help in time of need. He forgives and cleanses when we confess our sins and commit our lives to Christ (I John 1: 7, 9).

V. I-nstruction for Direction

"I will instruct thee and teach thee in the way which thou shalt go" (Ps. 32:8).

A. God's promises are of no avail to people who are set in their own ways and reject God's instruction.

B. Earnest Christians welcome God's instruction, knowing His direction is always best. God has promised to lead — we need only to follow (Prov. 3:5-6).

VI. S-trength in Weakness

"I will strengthen thee; yea, I will help thee" (Isa. 41:10).

A. Finite strength is limited and often fails, but God's infinite power never fails. So why do we persist in depending on our own limitations?

B. Little children are aware of their lack of strength and depend on their parents. Our heavenly Parent promises strength to His trusting children (Isa. 40:29).

VII. E-scape in Temptation

"God . . . will with the temptation also make a way to escape" (I Cor. 10:13).

A. When Jesus was tempted in the wilderness, He used the Word of God to defeat Satan. We must do likewise.

B. God promises victory in temptation to those who use His Word and pray (Matt. 26:41).

VIII. S-ecurity for the Future

"I go to prepare a place for you . . . . I will come again, and receive you unto myself" (John 14:2-3).

A. Security is sought in power, pleasure, and possessions, but Christ alone gives real and lasting security.

B. Christ's security is everlasting. There will be no more sin, sickness, suffering, or sorrow, "for the former things are passed away" (Rev. 21:4).

7

5-08-03 PM

Requirements for God's W-O-R-K

"What doth the Lord require of thee, but to do justly, and to love mercy, and to walk humbly with thy God" (Mic. 6:8).

God's work is most important. Christians please Him when they accept responsibility in His vineyard.

I. W-illing Workers

"Be rich in good works, ready to distribute, willing to communicate" (I Tim. 6:18).

A. Failure to do God's work or doing His work begrudgingly — both are patterns of behavior displeasing to God.

B. To love God is to willingly serve Him, whether by attendance at worship services, with our tithes and offerings, or by relaying His love to our fellowman as we have opportunity.

C. God loves willing workers. If we love Him we will do His work with joy and enthusiasm. It is our privilege, "for we are labourers together with God" (I Cor. 3:9).

II. O-bedient Workers

"I was not disobedient unto the heavenly vision" (Acts 26:19).

A. Obedience to God is shown by yielding our way to His and by pursuing spiritual maturity rather than personal gain.

B. Obedient workers seek God's will through prayer and studying the Bible. They act upon what God tells them to do.

C. We cannot be in bondage to self-will and also seek to obey God and do that which is pleasing to Him (I John 3:22).

III. R-ededicated Workers

"Present your bodies a living sacrifice, holy, acceptable unto God" (Rom. 12:1).

A. Neglect of God's work is a product of today's greedy world. Lives are engulfed in personal interests and fancies.

B. Christians who rededicate themselves to doing God's work discover that their own needs are supplied as they give God first place in their lives (Phil. 4:19).

IV. K-ingdom Workers

"Inherit the kingdom prepared for you. . . . Inasmuch as ye have done it unto the least of these my brethren, ye have done it unto me" (Matt. 25:34, 40).

A. Christians sometimes become involved in God's work for personal gain — social or political. If so, they have received their reward.

B. When we sincerely work for God we may receive criticism from others, but we must be faithful in doing our best, leaving the outcome to God.

C. We must be kingdom workers, assisting the poor and needy, visiting the sick and lonely, and seeking to bring the lost to a saving knowledge of Jesus Christ (Matt. 10:7, 8, 32).

8

The Love of God

Scripture: Romans 8:35-39
"Behold, what manner of love the Father hath bestowed upon us, that we should be called the sons of God" (I John 3:1).

Since God's love is the greatest force in the world, we should learn more about its working.

I. **The Challenge of Love**
"Who shall separate us from the love of Christ? shall tribulation, or distress . . . or peril, or sword?" (Rom. 8:35).
A. Christians are subject to discouragement and disappointment, as are all humans. God's love makes the difference — in outlook, strength, and endurance.
B. Christians can accept life's challenges with the assurance that God never fails. He is wisdom. He is power. He is love.

II. **The Conflict of Love**
"For thy sake we are killed all the day long; we are accounted as sheep for the slaughter" (Rom. 8:36).
A. In his quest for victory, Satan endeavors to diminish the power of God's love through deception.
B. God's omnipotent love brings victory over conflict. There is no defense against God's love. It always wins.

III. **The Conquest of Love**
"Nay, in all these things we are more than conquerors through him that loved us" (Rom. 8:37).
A. Christians often go down in defeat because they try to make it on their own strength when trouble, trial, and testing strike. They fail to depend on God's love.
B. God's love knows no defeat. No mountain is too steep, no valley too deep. "We are more than conquerors through him that loved us" (Rom. 8:37).

IV. **The Confidence of Love**
"I am persuaded, that neither death, nor life . . . nor things present, nor things to come . . ." (Rom. 8:38).

A. The apostle Paul was confident in God's love. He knew that it would endure through any and every situation.

B. We also must be confident in God's love. Our heavenly Father has revealed His great love for us through Jesus Christ (I John 3:1).

V. The Constancy of Love

". . .Nor any other creature, shall be able to separate us from the love of God" (Rom. 8:39).

A. People make excuses for lack of faith, hope, and love. God's love is constant and sure always.

B. How marvelous is the assurance that there is absolutely nothing that can come between us and the love of God unless we ourselves allow it.

9

The M-E-R-C-Y of God

"For as the heaven is high above the earth, so great is his mercy toward them that fear him" (Ps. 103:11).

We miserably fail to comprehend the extent of God's M-E-R-C-Y. May we reach a somewhat better understanding as we consider the following Scriptures.

I. M-otivates

"Who redeemeth thy life from destruction; who crowneth thee with lovingkindness and tender mercies" (Ps. 103:4).

A. There is much injustice and inequality in the world; greed and graft have crowded out liberty and justice.

B. God's mercy motivated Christ to come to earth to bring pardon and purpose to all mankind (Gal. 2:20).

C. We must be motivated by God's mercy to lift up the fallen, love the unloved, and introduce to everyone the abundant life through Christ (Ps. 108:4).

II. E-ndures

"For his mercy endureth forever" (Ps. 136:1-26).

A. We live in a materialistic world with treasures that do not last. They wear out, rust out, decay.

B. God's mercy is enduring: not for just a day, week, month, or year, but forever.

C. No sin is too great, no burden too heavy, no valley too deep, no suffering too severe, no night too long. God's mercy offers balm and healing (Ps. 100:5).

III. R-edeems

"According to his mercy he saved us, by the washing of regeneration, and renewing of the Holy Ghost" (Titus 3:5).

A. For his sin man deserves to die. "The wages of sin is death." No sacrifice could earn his pardon. Mankind was doomed.

B. In God's mercy we are rescued from our dilemma, for "the gift of God is eternal life through Jesus Christ our Lord" (Rom. 6:23). Christ died for our sins (I Cor. 15:3).

C. When we confess our sins and commit our life to Christ, we are forgiven, cleansed, and renewed in God's love (I John 1:9).

IV. C-omforts

"The Lord is very pitiful, and of tender mercy" (James 5:11).

A. God comforts the bereaved, the suffering, and the lonely. He consoles us when we pray. He proves His faithfulness when we test His promises. The Lord's mercy toward us is tender.

B. We are channels through which God's compassionate mercy flows to others (II Cor. 1:4).

V. Y-ields

"The fruit of the Spirit is love, joy, peace, longsuffering, gentleness, goodness, faith" (Gal. 5:22).

A. Christ came to destroy the works of the devil and to bring forth the fruit of the Spirit. His love lifts and gives life to those who receive Him.

B. We must cultivate the fruits of the Spirit. We must show mercy by performing good deeds, showing kindness, being understanding, sharing Christ with the unsaved, and promoting God's cause and kingdom here on earth (John 15:5).

10

God's Double Blessings

"Blessed be the God and Father of our Lord Jesus Christ, who hath blessed us with all spiritual blessings" (Eph. 1:3).

God loves us so much that He sends double blessings to His children.

I. He Forgives and Forgets

"In whom we have . . . the forgiveness of sins" (Eph. 1:7). "And their sins . . . will I remember no more" (Heb. 10:17).

A. Many profess to forgive, but they do not forget. They hold on to resentments which hurt and destroy.

B. We must forgive and also forget. If we do not forgive others, neither will our heavenly Father forgive us (Matt. 6:15).

C. God forgives and forgets. All who believe on the Lord Jesus Christ and repent of their sins receive this double blessing.

II. He Sanctifies and Satisfies

"The very God of peace sanctify you wholly; and . . . your whole spirit and soul and body be preserved blameless" (I Thess. 5:23). "He . . . filleth the hungry soul with goodness" (Ps. 107:9).

A. Christians must make a total commitment to God. They must not hold in reserve a portion of their lives for selfish purposes.

B. Those who completely surrender themselves to God are sanctified, cleansed, and filled with the Holy Spirit.

C. Discontent and dissatisfaction abound in today's troubled world. God's double blessings sanctify and satisfy His obedient children.

III. He Teaches and Touches

"I will . . . teach thee in the way which thou shalt go" (Ps. 32:8). "And Jesus . . . touched him" (Matt. 8:3).

A. Many people are unteachable. They insist on exerting their own will and going their own way. They fail in their pursuits to please God.

B. God's blessings are bestowed on those who heed His admonitions and seek His direction (Prov. 3:5).

C. When we trust God implicitly, He touches us physically, mentally, and spiritually.

IV. He Reassures and Will Receive (Us)

"Let not your heart be troubled . . . I go to prepare a place for you. And . . . I will . . . receive you unto myself" (John 14:1-3).

A. Today's world is filled with danger, frustration, and insecurity. Millions are seeking peace and security.

B. Real and lasting peace and security are found only in Jesus Christ. All who receive Him as Saviour and Lord are secure in the family of God.

C. Christ has promised to come again and receive us. When this happens there will be no more sin, sorrow, sickness, or suffering (Rev. 21:4).

11

God's Gifts to His Children

"For the wages of sin is death; but the gift of God is eternal life through Jesus Christ our Lord" (Rom. 6:23).

Parents give gifts to their children. They may give the best they can afford, but none can compare to God's gifts to His children.

I. God Gives Salvation

"For God so loved the world, that he gave his only begotten Son, that whosoever believeth in him should not perish, but have everlasting life" (John 3:16).

A. Salvation cannot be earned or purchased. It is God's free gift to those who accept His Son as Lord of their life.

B. To receive the gift of salvation we must believe on the Lord Jesus Christ and repent of our sins. We are forgiven and received into the family of God (Eph. 2:8).

C. When we make a total commitment of our will to God's will, the Holy Spirit dwells in us and produces the fruit of God's love.

II. God Gives Stability

"But the God of all grace . . . make you perfect, stablish, strengthen, settle you" (I Peter 5:10).

A. Some Christians are unstable in their spiritual life, sometimes up and sometimes down.

B. God wants His children to be trustworthy and faithful in all things; in their worship in God's house and in tithes and offerings.

C. We must accept God's gift of stability with devotion, determination, and diligence. God will teach, instruct, and direct us in the way we should go (Ps. 32:8).

III. God Gives Serenity

"And the peace of God . . . shall keep your hearts and minds through Christ Jesus" (Phil. 4:7).

A. Our world is seeking desperately to find peace of mind and spirit. Education, psychology, philosophies, and even war have failed to bring real and lasting peace.

B. Serenity is one of God's gifts to His children. He forgives their sins, cleanses their hearts, and carries their burdens. They should be at peace with God, themselves, and others.

C. God's peace is given to us. It cannot be bought, fought, or caught, but simply accepted through faith (John 14:27).

IV. God Gives Security

"But my God shall supply all your need according to his riches in glory by Christ Jesus" (Phil. 4:19).

A. Millions are seeking security in possessions, pleasure, and power. Today's affluent and permissive society has less security and more frustration than ever.

B. Belonging to the family of God gives the security of being heirs of God and joint heirs with Jesus Christ. He has promised to supply all our needs (Phil. 4:19).

C. God's children are secure in this life and in the life to come. Christ has gone to prepare a place for them and has promised to return and receive them unto Himself (John 14:1-3).

12

God Solves Problems

"The righteous cry, and the Lord heareth, and delivereth them out of all their troubles" (Ps. 34:17).

Problems are universal; everyone has them. Many try to solve their problems by themselves. Others seek help from friends or professionals. God is the supreme problem solver — He never fails.

I. The Problem of Sin
"For the wages of sin is death; but the gift of God is eternal life through Jesus Christ our Lord" (Rom. 6:23).
- A. Sin became man's Number One problem when he first became disobedient to God. Man could not save himself; angels could not atone for his sins. Only Jesus Christ could — and did.
- B. Christ paid the death penalty for the sins of all mankind. Everyone who receives Him as Saviour and Lord will be saved.

II. The Problem of Surrender
"He is able to keep that which I have committed unto him against that day" (II Tim. 1:12).
- A. Many Christians fail to receive the promises and blessings of God because they do not surrender. They persistently hold a portion of their life in reserve for selfish purposes.
- B. Surrender is total commitment of our will to God's will. The surrendered ones are filled with the Holy Spirit and thus receive God's blessing and become a blessing to others.

III. The Problem of Suffering
"If we suffer, we shall also reign with him: if we deny him, he also will deny us" (II Tim. 2:12).
- A. Suffering comes to everyone. It is the suffering endured for the cause of Christ that brings the reward of reigning with Him.
- B. God has a purpose in what He allows. When suffering strikes, we must be prayerful, patient, and seek God's pur-

pose, committing the keeping of our soul to Him (I Peter 4:19).

IV. The Problem of Sorrow

"As sorrowful, yet always rejoicing" (II Cor. 6:10).

A. Sorrow is universal. Bereavement, loneliness, and disappointment come to all. Some become despondent and give up when sorrow strikes.

B. Trust the Lord in time of sorrow. He can help us most. Through sorrow God teaches and touches, directs and delivers those who cast their care on Him (I Peter 5:7).

V. The Problem of Service

"For the love of Christ constraineth us . . . that they which live should not . . . live unto themselves" (II Cor. 5:14-15).

A. Professing Christians often "live unto themselves." Their time is occupied with making money and having a good time. Love for God and concern for others is lacking.

B. Our love for God is shown by doing His work through His power. He will go with us as we help the needy, visit the sick and lonely, and share Christ with the lost. When we yield our best, God will do the rest. He is able and willing to solve our every problem (II Cor. 6:1).

13

Where Is the Joy?

"Restore unto me the joy of thy salvation" (Ps. 51:12).

Have the cares of life and the chaotic condition of our world caused us to lose the joy of our salvation? We can pray with the psalmist, "Restore unto me the joy of thy salvation."

I. Pardon for Sins

"There is joy in the presence of the angels of God over one sinner that repenteth" (Luke 15:10).

A. "Oh, the joy of sins forgiv'n! Oh, the bliss the Bloodwashed know! Oh, the peace akin to heav'n, Where the healing waters flow!" (Verse 1 of the hymn, "The Healing Waters.")

B. Forgiveness brings freedom from the bondage of sin, from guilt, and fear of the judgment. But where is the joy of pardon?

C. Resentments, guilt (real or false), neglect of God's Word, and overwork cause a lack of joy. When we lay these humbly before the Lord and pray, "Restore unto me the joy of thy salvation" He will (I Peter 1:8).

II. Purity in Spirit

"And the disciples were filled with joy, and with the Holy Spirit" (Acts 13:52).

A. Christian joy depends upon a total commitment to God — no holding in reserve of certain favorite possessions or pursuits.

B. Complete surrender to God releases us from worry. God holds the future. He holds us. The responsibility of our lives belongs to Him.

C. Through total commitment the Holy Spirit fills us with God's love. Loving God and others restores to us the joy of salvation (Acts 15:9).

III. Peace of Soul

"The kingdom of God is not meat and drink; but . . . peace, and joy in the Holy Ghost" (Rom. 14:17).

A. Today's world is seeking for peace, trying to attain serenity and security with power, possessions, and pleasure.

B. Human endeavor can never bring satisfaction to the longing soul. Psychologists say that man's basic needs are "the need to belong" and "the need for reasonable security."

C. Christians "belong" to the King of kings, who supplies our needs and promises eternal life. We rejoice because in Christ we have peace of mind and soul (Phil. 4:7).

IV. Power for Service

"Serve the Lord with gladness: come before his presence with singing" (Ps. 100:2).

A. When Christians neglect, make excuses, or flatly refuse to participate in performing God's work, where is the joy?

B. Christians are endued by the Holy Spirit with power for service. In doing God's work we receive the joy of the Lord (Acts 1:8).

C. To know the Lord, to have assurance of our salvation, to claim His love and His promises, to serve Him with tithes, and to reflect His love to others — this is where the joy of salvation is found (Heb. 12:2).

14

What It Means to Be "Born Again"

"Except a man be born again, he cannot see the kingdom of God" *(John 3:3).*

The term "born again" is used much too indiscriminately. The following attributes belong to those who have indeed experienced the "New Birth."

I. Redeemed
"In whom we have redemption through his blood, the forgiveness of sins" (Eph. 1:7).

A. Mankind was alienated from God because of his disobedience. The penalty for man's sin was death.

B. Christ paid our penalty for sin with His death on the cross. Man's fellowship with God could thus be restored; he was redeemed from the death sentence.

C. When we repent of our sins and by faith accept Christ as Saviour and Lord of our lives, we are "born again" (Col. 1:14).

II. Received
"And if children, then heirs; heirs of God, and joint-heirs with Christ" (Rom. 8:17).

A. "Born-again" Christians still make blunders, but they are not rejected or disinherited for their faults and failures.

B. When we are "born again," we are received, accepted, and loved into the family of God through Jesus Christ.

C. Only the children of God can feel the warmth and security that the Holy Spirit brings to those who are "born again" (Gal. 4:6-7).

III. **Reformed**

"Old things are passed away; behold, all things are become new" (II Cor. 5:17).

A. Those who profess to be "born again" but continue in the old lustful, lewd, and sinful life are deceiving themselves, misrepresenting Christ to others, and displeasing God. To be "born again" is to forsake sin.

B. "Born-again" Christians have a new life. "Old things are passed away." They desire to please God; they delight in His way, Word, will, and work.

IV. **Released**

"If the Son therefore shall make you free, ye shall be free indeed" (John 8:36).

A. Some profess to be "born again," but they are still bound by social pressures and opinions of friends. They try to hold to God with one hand and the world with the other (Matt. 6:24).

B. When "born-again" Christians make a total commitment to God, they are cleansed, released from the bondage of sin to rejoice in the Lord (Gal. 5:1).

V. **Rewarded**

"Be thou faithful unto death, and I will give thee a crown of life" (Rev. 2:10).

A. "Born-again" Christians are rewarded here and now; they are forgiven, cleansed, accepted, and freed.

B. The Christian life is the most happy and rewarding way to live.

C. The "born again" will be rewarded in the life to come, also. They will receive the crown of life and live eternally with the Lord (Ps. 73:24).

15

Ways to End Personality Conflicts

"Endeavouring to keep the unity of the Spirit in the bond of peace" (Eph. 4:3).

It is sometimes difficult to end personality conflicts. Prayer, love, and effort go a long way toward resolving conflicts. The following elements are also necessary.

I. Courtesy
   "Be courteous" (I Peter 3:8).
   A. Christians should not be discourteous toward those who disagree with them; they should neither shun them or treat them rudely.
   B. Consideration of the rights and feelings of others is only the beginning of Christian love.
   C. Courtesy with kindness and respect is a major step toward bringing an end to personality conflicts (Heb. 10:24).

II. Compassion
   "Be ye all of one mind, having compassion one of another" (I Peter 3:8).
   A. When compassion is lacking, resentments easily take hold. Have you heard anyone pray *at* others instead of *for* them? Their personality conflicts increase.
   B. Compassion and understanding are essential Christian qualities. Empathy is the key to more love for others. Empathy is "walking a day in their moccasins."
   C. Compassion, sincere prayer, and a forgiving spirit drive away resentments and personality conflicts (Eph. 4:32).

III. Compromise
   "If it be possible, as much as lieth in you, live peaceably with all men" (Rom. 12:18).
   A. People who are set in their ways, stubbornly clinging to their own ideas regardless of the effect upon others, are unhappy and have many conflicts.

B. To have friends, we must be congenial and friendly. We must be pliable — willing to compromise when an issue doesn't violate our convictions.

C. When each is willing to "give a little," disagreements can usually be resolved (I Peter 5:5).

IV. **Christlikeness**
"Walk in love, as Christ also hath loved us, and hath given himself for us" (Eph. 5:2).

A. Christ did everything from the basis of love. He healed the sick; restored sight to the blind; made the lame to walk; forgave sins. He loved so much that He gave His life for us.

B. To be Christlike we must walk in His love, sharing Christ by giving of ourselves — "such as I have give I thee: In the name of Jesus Christ" (Acts 3:6).

C. Christlikeness is the most effective way to end personality conflicts. There is no defense against love, for "[love] shall cover the multitude of sins" (I Peter 4:8).

16

You Get What You Give

"Give, and it shall be given unto you; . . . . For with the same measure that ye mete withal it shall be measured to you again" (Luke 6:38).

This text is used in reference to giving and receiving money, but applies also to greater values.

I. **Consideration**
"Put on . . . mercies, kindness, humbleness . . . Forbearing . . . and forgiving one another" (Col. 3:12-13).

A. The kind of seeds a farmer sows determines the kind of harvest he will reap.

B. The spiritual seed we plant also determines the harvest. If we are considerate of the feelings and needs of others, we will usually receive kindness and appreciation in return.

C. Consideration for others brings God's blessing. God forgives us as we forgive (Matt. 6:13-14). He is pleased when we love one another.

II. Consolation
"That we may be able to comfort them . . . by the comfort wherewith we ourselves are comforted of God" (II Cor. 1:4).

A. God comforts His children, enabling us to be comforters to others.

B. We receive God's blessings when we reach out with compassion to the bereaved, the lonely, the troubled and depressed.

C. God consoles Christians with His presence. He never leaves nor forsakes them (Heb. 13:5). He consoles with His peace (Phil. 4:7).

III. Cooperation
"For we are labourers together with God" (I Cor. 3:9).

A. Independence is no longer a virtue when it creates difficulty in working with God and others because we insist on doing things our way.

B. To receive the benefits of congeniality, we must work together in harmony and unity of spirit (Ps. 133:1).

C. As laborers with God we help in the work of the church and assist wherever we find opportunity (Eph. 4:2-3).

IV. Confidence
"And this is the confidence that we have in him, that, if we ask any thing according to his will, he heareth us" (I John 5:14).

A. Lack of faith is often expressed through pessimistic attitudes that bring disappointment to self, discouragement to others, and displeasure to God (Heb. 11:6).

B We demonstrate faith by declaring our confidence in God. When we do, others will grow in faith through our influence.

C. The more we exercise our faith the more it will grow. Unused faith dwindles and dies (James 2:17-18).

17

The Prayers of Righteous Men Prevail

"The effective fervent prayer of a righteous man availeth much"
(James 5:16).

Prayer is a mighty force. God does things in answer to prayer that He would not do otherwise.

I. **Abraham Prayed with Commitment**
   "The angel of the Lord called . . . Abraham, Abraham: and he said, Here *am* I" (Gen. 22:11).
   A. Abraham's faith had been severely tested. When he prayed with commitment to the will of God, God intervened.
   B. When we commit our will totally to God's will, our prayers will prevail also (Rom. 12:1).

II. **Jacob Prayed Without Constraint**
   "As a prince hast thou power with God and with men, and hast prevailed" (Gen. 32:28).
   A. God told Jacob to return home, but he feared Esau. Jacob prayed with persistence and God answered (Gen. 32:26).
   B. We must touch God without constraint, also. God will answer when we prevail in prayer for ourselves and others.

III. **Moses Prayed with Concern**
   "If thou wilt forgive their sin — and if not, blot me. I pray thee, out of thy book which thou hast written" (Exod. 32:32).
   A. Because Israelites made idols, God threatened to destroy them. Moses intervened by putting his life on the line for them.
   B. The intervening prayer of concern for unconverted friends and loved ones God will hear and answer.

IV. **David Prayed with Contrition**
   "Have mercy upon me, O God . . . blot out my transgressions" (Ps. 51:1).
   A. When David repented of his sin with humility and contrition, God forgave and restored to him the joy of salvation.

B. Our prayers, also, must come from a humble and contrite heart. God will forgive; His mercy endures forever (Ps. 106:1).

V. Elijah Prayed with Confidence

"Hear me, O Lord . . . that this people may know that thou art . . . God. . . . Then the fire of the Lord fell" (I Kings 18:37-38).

A. Elijah prayed with faith to the true, living God. The fire fell, the rain came, the skeptics believed. Elijah's God answered prayer!

B. The prayer of faith will move God's hand to forgive, cleanse, remove mountains. He is the same miracle-working God who changes not (Mal. 3:6).

VI. Daniel Prayed with Courage

"Daniel . . . his windows being open . . . kneeled . . . and prayed . . . before his God" (Dan. 6:10).

A. Daniel did not buckle under threat. God honored his courageous devotion and faith, and protected him from the lions.

B. In the face of persecution our prayer of courageous faith also will be heard by God, who can deliver us as He did Daniel (Dan. 6:26, 27).

VII. Jesus Prayed with Compassion

"Father, forgive them; for they know not what they do" (Luke 23:34).

A. In Jesus' darkest and most excruciating hour, He prayed with compassion for those who crucified Him.

B. When we pray with compassion for those who despitefully use us, we too will learn to love them.

18

The Heavenly Highway

*"And an highway will be there, and a way, and it shall be callled
The way of holiness" (Isa. 35:8).*

Man has made the great thoroughfares of imperial Rome, the
magnificent highways of modern Europe, and the tremendous turn-
pikes and freeways of America. God has surpassed them all. Let us
note the features of the heavenly highway God has prepared for His
people.

I. **A Hallowed Way**
   "It shall be called The way of holiness; the unclean shall not
   pass over it" (Isa. 35:8).
   A. As we travel through life we are confronted with the choice
      between two ways — a "highway" or a "low way." Many
      travel the "low way" of self-seeking and sensuality, which
      leads finally to destruction.
   B. The "highway" is God's way of purity and truth. It progress-
      es through the infinite sunshine of God's love.
   C. This "hallowed highway" "shall be called The way of
      holiness." Those who totally commit their will to God are
      enabled by the Holy Spirit to travel the heavenly highway
      which leads to eternal life with the Lord.

II. **A Harmless Way**
   "No lion shall be there, nor any ravenous beast shall go up
   thereon . . ." (Isa. 35:9).
   A. Ours is a dangerous world. Theft, drug abuse, rape, and
      murder are common. Many homes are invaded by hatred,
      strife, separation, and divorce.
   B. Satan is going about as a roaring lion, seeking whom he can
      devour (I Peter 5:8). However, Christ is more than a match
      for the devil. We are conquerors through Him.
   C. Jesus Christ is the way. We can follow Him safely. Keep on
      praying, reading God's promises, working, trusting, and
      traveling on God's heavenly highway (Ps. 91:15).

III. **A Home Way**

"And the ransomed of the Lord shall return, and come to Zion with songs and everlasting joy upon their heads . . ." (Isa. 35:10).

A. Every road is good if it leads us home — no matter how rough, steep, or winding it may be. God's royal highway will take the Christian to his heavenly home.

B. There will be mountains of trial to climb, valleys of sorrow to descend. We may grow tired and footsore, but the trials of the road will seem insignificant at our journey's end.

C. The apostle Paul wrote, "For I reckon that the sufferings of the present time are not worthy to be compared with the glory which shall be revealed in us" (Rom. 8:18).

IV. **A Happy Way**

"They shall obtain joy and gladness, and sorrow and sighing shall flee away" (Isa. 35:10).

A. Happiness is often sought in the form of sinful pleasures and selfish possessions; but the happiness thus found is short-lived and disappointing.

B. We can find true happiness only as we find God. We cannot enjoy ourselves in the highest sense unless we enjoy God. He is the source of real and lasting happiness.

C. When we accept Christ as Saviour and Lord, we begin to travel the heavenly highway, which is God's happy way to life eternal. There joy and gladness shall reign "and sorrow and sighing shall flee away" (Isa. 35:10).

pample

19

Security in Christ

"These things I have spoken unto you, that in me ye might have peace. In the world ye shall have tribulation: but be of good cheer, I have overcome the world" (John 16:33).

Today's world is trying desperately to find security. Only in Christ can real security be found.

I. **Counsel**
"These things I have spoken unto you" (John 16:33).
   A. Counsel comes from many sources for financial, legal, marriage, and family problems. Besides professional counselors, newspapers, magazines, radio, and television offer counsel.
   B. Security sought from counsel is deceptive. Trusting ill-advised counsel may be a step from frying pan into fire.
   C. Real security results from Christ's counsel.

II. **Calmness**
"That in me ye might have peace" (John 16:33).
   A. Seeking peace of mind and heart through financial gain, learning, or psychology is fruitless.
   B. The record number of unhappy and broken homes in this generation does not give evidence of an atmosphere of peacefulness.
   C. The secret of peace of mind and calmness of spirit is found only in Jesus Christ (John 14:27).

III. **Conflict**
"In the world ye shall have tribulation" (John 16:33).
   A. Christians are not immune to trouble. Our world is filled with inescapable confict.
   B. Christians are in the world but not of the world. They are, however, Satan's hottest battlefield in the effort to defeat God's purpose.
   C. Christians are on the scene of conflict; they sail the troubled seas of life; but they are secure in Christ Jesus.

IV. Comfort

"But be of good cheer" (John 16:33).

A. Discouragement, despondency, and depression express much of today's general mood. Comfort and love are much-needed commodities.

B. In this life are many hurtful distractions and discouragements. Friends may let us down, illness may assail us, and burdens may seem too heavy. But Jesus never fails us.

C. Christ brings comfort to all who come to Him. He is still saying to the troubled, "Be of good cheer." Christ is our security.

V. Conquest

"I have overcome the world" (John 16:33).

A. Jesus suffered temptation, persecution, ridicule, and abuse. In spite of this He declared, "I have overcome the world."

B. We can do nothing through our own weak power, but we can overcome the world through Christ, for we are more than conquerors through Him.

C. Man's search for security by obtaining possessions, pleasures, and power has failed. Christians have real security in the present and lasting security in the life to come — through Christ (I Cor. 2:9).

20 preached 7-6-03 pm

Lessons from the Ants

Scripture: Proverbs 6:6-11
"Go to the ant, thou sluggard; consider her ways, and be wise" (Prov. 6:6).

The Bible teaches many lessons from nature and God's creation. We can learn some valuable lessons from the ants.

I. The Ants Teach Performance

"He that abideth in me, and I in him . . . bringeth forth much fruit" (John 15:5).

A. Ants are always busy, never lazy, never have to make excuses. We can learn performance from ants.
B. Failure to learn this lesson is seen in slackness toward doing God's work and too much involvement in personal activities.
C. No excuse is acceptable for Christians to refrain from working for God. God's fields are ready for harvest. We must labor in them today (Matt. 9:38).

II. The Ants Teach Preservation

"The ants are a people not strong, yet they prepare their meat in the summer" (Prov. 30:25).

A. Ants are thrifty creatures. They do not fritter away their summer days but work diligently, storing food for the rainy and winter days ahead.
B. Christians should learn this lesson of preservation, spending money and time wisely in preparation for the rainy days of recession, inflation, ill health, and old age.
C. It is most important that Christians store up treasure for eternal life, living for God and for others (Matt. 6:19-21).

III. The Ants Teach Participation

"As workers together with him" (II Cor. 6:1).

A. Ants seem to have no difficulty participating in tasks to be done. They work together in harmony, accomplishing their assignments.
B. Christians often fail to cooperate in accomplishing God's work, but sit with folded hands and engage in criticisms while others do the job.
C. God's love should constrain His children to work together with Him in unity, to participate in the greatest of all endeavors (II Cor. 5:14).

IV. The Ants Teach Perseverance

"But he that shall endure unto the end, the same shall be saved" (Matt. 24:13).

A. When their homes and possessions are completely destroyed, the ants begin to rebuild immediately. They persevere.
B. Contrary winds blow and storms leave destruction. When trouble, trials, and testings strike, Christians who have an all-powerful God need not despair.

C. We must persevere, whether our problems be of personal nature or in the cause of Christ. The Christian's greatest hope lies beyond this life. "Be thou faithful unto death, and I will give thee a crown of life" (Rev. 2:10).

21

It's a Must

"I must work the works of him that sent me, while it is day: the night cometh, when no man can work" (John 9:4).

To do God's work as we should, there are some "musts" to follow.

I. I Must Be Friendly
"A man that hath friends must shew himself friendly" (Prov. 18:24).
A. Many professing Christians are unfriendly, cold toward others because they are self-centered, perhaps conceited. Some are self-conscious.
B. Unfriendliness defeats one's Christianity, disappoints others, and displeases God.
C. I must exhibit God's love by exuding welcome, warmth, and understanding; only thus will I help create in others the desire to be Christians also (John 13:34).

II. I Must Be Forgiving
"If ye forgive not men their trespasses, neither will your Father forgive your trespasses" (Matt. 6:15).
A. As a Christian, I must forgive. I cannot live with resentments and grudges. They destroy my life physically, mentally, and spiritually.
B. God forgives only those who forgive others. Total surrender of our will to God's will enables us to be forgiving (Matt. 6:14).

III. I Must Be Fervent
"Fervent in spirit; serving the Lord" (Rom. 12:11).

A. Can a Christian be lethargic and lack concern for God's work — seldom attending His house of worship, using His tithe for selfish purposes, and spending His time for selfish pursuits?

B. "Fervent" means having great warmth of feeling, being intensely devoted or in earnest.

C. I must fervently expend my time, talent, and treasure on endeavors having eternal value (John 9:4).

IV. I Must Be Fruitful

"I have chosen you . . . that ye should go and bring forth fruit" (John 15:16).

A. Some may get excited when challenged to bear spiritual fruit but lose sight of their goal when their enthusiasm subsides. Their fruit is limited, their growth stunted.

B. When enthusiasm subsides and inspiration is lacking, it is evidence of the need to be renewed in God's Spirit.

C. I must be aware of the needs of others, to aid, to comfort, to lead the lost to a saving knowledge of Jesus Christ (Matt. 6:19-20).

V. I Must Be Faithful

"Be thou faithful unto death, and I will give thee a crown of life" (Rev. 2:10).

A. God isn't so concerned because Christians make mistakes, that we blunder, err, and fail at times.

B. God wants us to hold fast to Him when we are weak and trembling, to keep trusting and trying when we flounder, to get up when we fall and rely on His strength for accomplishment.

C. I must be faithful. I must persevere — never give up. I must keep on keeping on (Rev. 2:10).

22

Are You Pulling or Pushing?

"Whatsoever ye do, do all to the glory of God" (I Cor. 10:31).

God has a work for each of us. A positive and prayerful attitude will enable us to accomplish God's purpose for our life.

I. **The Downward Pull**
   A. Some who claim the name of Christ seldom speak a complimentary word, but continuously criticize and find fault.
   B. An inferiority complex, envy, or resentment strives to demean or discredit others in an effort to lift one's own sagging ego.
   C. Christians with "God confidence" need not pull others downward. Forgiveness, cleansing, love, and faith lift the estimation of one's worth.

II. **The Upward Push**
   A. Happy Christians push upward. Although aware of the world's chaotic condition, they look beyond discouraging circumstances with the eye of faith.
   B. Reach for the highest and best. Look for the good in others.
   C. We please God and help others by pushing upward in faith. Faith brings the victory (I John 5:4).

III. **The Inward Pull**
   A. Some Christians pull inward. They are self-centered, concerned only with personal interests.
   B. Some feel unwanted and unimportant. They fail to realize that God is no respecter of persons and loves each of us equally.
   C. Christians should not pull inward. God has given each of us certain talents or gifts. We must recognize our God-given abilities and develop them, using them to glorify God.

IV. **The Outward Push**
   A. Christians who push outward are fortunate. They lose themselves in service for God and others and find joy and blessing in so doing.

B. We push outward by helping those in need, comforting the sick and lonely, and sharing Christ.

C. Pushing outward is not only rewarding in this life; our efforts bring rewards in the life to come.

V. The Backward Pull

A. Christians sometimes pull backward. They lack a vision for progress. This discourages others and hinders the advancement of God's Kingdom on earth.

B. We must cooperate with God, His cause, and His people. "We . . . as workers together with [God] . . ." (II Cor. 6:1) must approve ourselves as "ministers of God" (II Cor. 6:4).

C. We must not hinder God's work by pulling backward.

VI. The Forward Push

A. Victorious Christians push forward. When the mountains are steep and the valleys deep, they continue to push ahead — they never stop.

B. We must push forward when results are slow coming in. As we continue to be faithful, God will send the increase in His own time and way.

C. "Be thou faithful unto death, and I will give thee a crown of life" (Rev. 2:10).

23

Be Your . . . Own Person

"Greater is he that is in you, than he that is in the world" (I John 4:4).

What God wants for you may be different from what He wants for others. Each person must strive to be what God wants him to be.

I. Think What God Wants YOU to Think

A. Think positively. Replace negative thoughts with optimism and faith (Phil. 4:8).

B. Nurture pure thoughts. Think often of God's holiness, greatness, and goodness. Ask God to help you think what He wants you to think (Ps. 33:5).

II. See What God Wants YOU to See
A. See the good in others. Overlook the faults and failures of others, remembering that we all have them (I Peter 4:8).
B. Look for ways to assist others. See the helpless or lonely person to whom you can lend a helping hand. Do not look at the difficult situation, but at the opportunity to serve. See what God wants you to see (Heb. 12:15).

III. Hear What God Wants YOU to Hear
A. Christians become spiritually drained listening to the loud, lewd, and lust-filled presentations on television, radio, and theater, which are degenerating our nation's morals and displeasing God.
B. Jesus listened with compassion to the inner cries of the sinful, suffering, and sorrowful. We should do likewise. Hear what God wants you to hear (Mark 4:24).

IV. Say What God Wants YOU to Say
A. Harsh, unkind, and critical words have no place in the Christian's conversation.
B. Let Christ speak through you. He offers words of love, faith, comfort, understanding, and forgiveness (Luke 6:45).

V. Do What God Wants YOU to Do
A. Many Christians are too busy with selfish pursuits. Their personal activities cause them to neglect God and God's work.
B. We must make room in our schedules for God, giving Him first place in our life (Col. 1:18).

VI. Go Where God Wants YOU to Go
A. Despite gas problems, people are on-the-go. Our world is on wheels, following after selfish pleasures and pursuits.
B. Christians should go for God — to His house to worship and to the homes of others to witness (John 15:16). God offers to direct us to the right places and persons. Ask Him where He wants you to go (Isa. 48:17).

24

Christ and Heaven

"Eye hath not seen, nor ear heard, neither have entered into the heart of man, the things which God hath prepared for them that love him" (I Cor. 2:9).

Christ is the link between mankind and heaven. His death on the cross made it possible for us to be brought back to God.

I. **Christ Proceeded from Heaven**
   "The first man is of the earth, earthy: the second man is the Lord from heaven" (I Cor. 15:47).
   A. Christ was involved in the creation of the heavens and earth, the fowl of the air, fish of the sea, beasts of the forests, and the crown of creation, mankind.
   B. The penalty of death was placed on mankind when he disobeyed God.
   C. Because of God's love for mankind, Christ proceeded from heaven to pay the penalty for our sins once and for all (John 3:13-15).

II. **Christ Preached About Heaven**
   "Lay not up for yourselves treasures upon earth . . . but lay up for yourselves treasures in heaven . . ." (Matt. 6:19-20).
   A. While Christ was on earth He preached about heaven. He taught us how to get there. He promised we would be rewarded by laying up treasures in heaven.
   B. Christ discouraged placing too much value on temporal things. He admonished us to "seek ye first the kingdom of God . . . and all these things shall be added unto you" (Matt. 6:33).
   C. Christ promised heaven to those who overcome (Rev. 3:21).

III. **Christ Purchased Us for Heaven**
   "But now in Christ Jesus ye . . . are made nigh by the blood of Christ" (Eph. 2:13).
   A. Mankind became alienated from God when he sinned. Jesus Christ brought reconciliation when He paid sin's penalty for mankind on the cross of Calvary (Col. 1:21-22; John 3:16).

B. We now can receive forgiveness and cleansing when we believe on the Lord Jesus Christ, repent, and confess our sin. (I John 1:9).

IV. Christ Is Preparing Heaven for Us

"I go to prepare a place for you . . . I will come again, and receive you unto myself" (John 14:2-3)

A. Before Christ left the earth He promised to go and prepare a place where there will be no more sin, suffering, or sorrow for those who love Him (Rev. 21:4). He also promised to return and receive them unto Himself.

B. For nearly two thousand years Christ has been preparing heaven for us. If it took only six days to create the earth by His omnipotent power, how much more beautiful must heaven be!

C. Christ is coming soon. Since we want our loved ones and friends to go to heaven, too, we must keep praying, believing, and working.

25

A Good Example

Scripture: Luke 10:25-37
"Go, and do thou likewise" (Luke 10:37).

The Good Samaritan is a type of Christ. Following his example — loving God and our neighbor — is the mark of the Christian.

I. The Caring of Love

"And when he saw him, he had compassion on him" (Luke 10:33).

A. The priest and Levite passed the man who had been robbed and brutally beaten. The Good Samaritan had compassion on him and went to him.

B. Christ came to seek and save that which was lost (Luke 19:10). He does not pass by or look the other way. He comes to us with love and compassion.

C. We too must go with compassion and love to the needy, the hurt, and the unsaved.

II. The Bearing of Love

"And went to him, and bound up his wounds . . . and brought him to an inn" (Luke 10:34).

A. The Good Samaritan didn't stop with expressing sympathy for the man. He gave every possible aid.

B. Christ always helps those who are His. He lifts the fallen, heals the sick, and forgives the sinner. He bore our sins upon the cross with love.

C. In true Christian compassion, we also are to bear one another's burdens (Gal. 6:2), becoming unselfishly involved in the needs of others.

III. The Sharing of Love

"He took out two pence, and gave them to the host, and said unto him, Take care of him" (Luke 10:35).

A. The Good Samaritan shared his time, talent, and treasure. He denied himself to help the man in distress.

B. Christ made the supreme sacrifice for lost mankind. He paid for our sins with His life's blood. Christ gave His all.

C. "Love isn't love until we give it away." Our time, talent, and treasure are given us to light the world, bearing Christ's love, comfort, and hope wherever we go.

IV. The Daring of Love

"Then said Jesus unto him, Go, and do thou likewise" (Luke 10:37).

A. It took courage for the Good Samaritan to become involved. Those who did not help the stranger were afraid of complicating their own lives with someone else's problems.

B. Christ became involved, daring to die for mankind because He loved (John 3:16). Love is courageous and conquers (I Cor. 13:7-8).

C. Love demands courage. We must be ready to follow the example of Christ — and the Good Samaritan. There is no defense against love; it always wins.

26

With Christ in the Home

"I am come that they might have life, and that they might have it more abundantly" (John 10:10).

Many homes are unhappy because they do not have Christ. He makes all the difference — He brings abundant life.

I. Home Is a Place for Living
"By a new and living way, which he hath consecrated for us" (Heb. 10:20).
  - A. Many of today's homes, without Christ, are little more than a place to eat, sleep, and park the cars.
  - B. Christ makes the difference. His presence in the home encourages prayer and direction for a worthwhile life.
  - C. Christian homes are not places of mere existence; they afford communication, companionship, and happy, meaningful relationships (John 10:10).

II. Home Is a Place with Liberty
"If the Son therefore shall make you free, ye shall be free indeed" (John 8:36).
  - A. Many houses are like prisons where the occupants are bound with the chains of sin. Christ stands at the door and knocks, desiring entrance.
  - B. When the door is opened to Him, Christ breaks the chains of sin. He brings forgiveness and sets us free from Satan's bondage.
  - C. When Christ comes into the home, He breaks down walls of resentment, hatred, jealousy, and strife. He brings peace, love, and joy (John 8:32).

III. Home Is a Place for Lifting
"Who comforteth us . . . that we may be able to comfort them which are in any trouble" (II Cor. 1:4).
  - A. The world is filled with selfishness and self-centeredness. Each person is looking out for himself only.
  - B. Everyone needs a lift at times. Christian families should help one another; each member should be ready to lend a helping hand and lighten the burden of another.

C. Christ's presence encourages practice of this admonition: "And let us consider one another to provoke unto love and to good works" (Heb. 10:24).

IV. **Home Is a Place With Love**
"Beloved, let us love one another: for love is of God" (I John 4:7).
A. Homes where love is lacking are sad and lonely, especially when children are involved. Everyone needs to love and be loved. It is a built-in psychological and spiritual need.
B. God loved the world so much He sent Christ to bring us love. Christ brings understanding, compassion, and love to the home.
C. Families that have the love of Christ will never be completely separated, for God is love and He is eternal. Love conquers the conflicts in this life, and love will reign in the life to come (I Cor. 13:13).

27

The Qualities of a Good Mother
(Mother's Day)

"Her children arise up, and call her blessed" (Prov. 31:28).

A good mother is like Christ in many ways. She is more concerned about the well-being of her children than her own.

I. **She Is Loyal**
A. A good mother is loyal, faithful to support her children however difficult the situation.
B. God's loyalty to His children is supreme. Through love He gave His Son to suffer and die for us, paying our ransom (I John 1:9; 4:9).
C. Love and loyalty go hand in hand. Gratefully acknowledge God's goodness; uphold and encourage the good in our fellowmen.

II. She Listens

A. A good mother listens to her children; she is concerned about their problems. They can talk to her in confidence; she offers solace and understanding.

B. God hears the faintest cry of the least of His saints. He understands our deepest needs (I Peter 5:7).

C. God speaks through His promises. God also uses the gifts of others to make known to us His will and His wisdom. We do well to heed God's Word and the wise counsel of other Christians.

III. She Lifts

A. A good mother not only listens to her children but uplifts them. She sacrificially lightens the burdens of her children.

B. The Lord also uplifts His children; He helps them over the rough places, guides them in darkness, and supplies their needs (Phil. 4:19).

C. God will use us to lift others — to share with the less fortunate, care for the sick and lonely, and witness to the unsaved.

IV. She Laughs

A. A good mother laughs with her children. She wants them to be happy and joyful. They enjoy being with her as they work and play together.

B. God also rejoices with His children. Christ endured the cross for the joy that was set before Him (Heb. 12:2).

C. Christians should rejoice in the Lord. Happiness is attractive. Others will want to know Christ when they see the joy of the Lord in us (Phil. 4:4).

V. She Loves

A. A good mother's love for her children is surpassed only, perhaps, by the love of God. Her children respond with their love in return.

B. God's love is the greatest love possible (I John 3:1). He gave His only begotten Son to die for us in evidence of that love.

C. Love is a built-in psychological and spiritual need. God's love reaches out through us to meet that need in the world (I John 3:16-18).